# Stepping Over Seasons

## Ashley Capes

*Stepping Over Seasons*
Copyright © 2017

First published by Interactive Press 2009

Cover: www.vividcovers.com
Layout & Typset: Close-Up Books

All rights reserved. No part of this book may be reproduced in any form by any electronic or mechanical means including photocopying, recording, or information storage and retrieval without permission in writing from the authors.

ISBN-978-0-9876232-0-1

Published by Close-Up Books
Melbourne, Australia

*For Brooke*

## acknowledgements

I would like to thank the editors of the following journals and anthologies where some of the following poems have appeared or are forthcoming.

*Mascara Literary Review, Red Leaves, Island, Stylus Poetry Journal, otoliths, Pendulum, Speedpoets, miel magazine, ARTrocity, Extempore, foam:e, Bluepepper, Poems & Pieces, verb-ate-him, The Tasmanian Times, Westerly*

'farm' was runner up in the 2008 Ipswich Poetry Feast Open Poetry Section

'bianca' was commended in the 2008 MPU Poetry Competition

I would also like to thank the following people, whose careful consideration and input have made this collection so much stronger: David Reiter, Anna Bartlett and Jeremy Green at IP, Michelle Cahill, Graham Nunn and Simon Cooper for their advice and insight, both my families for their support, and my wife for everything, thank you.

2017 Edition:

Thanks for taking a look at this new edition!

Ashley Capes' poetry is unique for its post-haiku fusion of imagery, for its sensitivity to detail, both commonplace and nuanced. The poems move indirectly through personal moments of adversity and unease in the home and the suburban world, in which they are located. A promising and unsentimental collection.

*Michelle Cahill*

## contents

other objects
all this ink
august rain
beached
shell
bianca
farm
woodsmoke
slow moon
mushrooms
the pull of engines
overlook
tar and white paint
harold
small town
leaking
late night
sunrise today
it would be unfair to say
how green wood burns
on the road
october
moonlight
little frontiers
alpine road
kakashi
take five
fujin's bag
white butterfly
dive-bombing
ashoka
orion's belt
echidna
black comedy

*Stepping Over Seasons*

bukowski and a wide range of landlords
eastern avenue
bitches brew
autumn-house
botanic
royal on the park
grass seeds
by the curve
the jacket

2017

Author's Note
Additional Poems

## other objects

my wedding ring is a plain silver
barrel band. same as dad's, very modest
and very hard to keep smooth,
with scratches I can't keep track of and
don't want to hide. it's no good pretending
the marriage is perfect, no use
hanging all our memories and every
step of the future on just one symbol. other
objects speak of love, too. the weeping
maple we've shifted to every house, the
cup we fill with knives and forks
or the handwritten address you gave me
the night we met, walking the city
and flinging orange peel into hedges, things
that endure, things that have lines
and marks to prove them.

## all this ink

if I sit up tonight
and stifle my yawns with music
and if I write something
worthwhile, maybe I can take her
where the sky is cracked
ice, and it's beautiful
because we're together.
if I sit up tonight
arms cold, torso wrong
and typing about it,
rented, everything rented
maybe I'll come up with a way.
if I sit up tonight and all this ink
becomes poetry, I could point the wheel
to a place we've never been,
watch Venice sink a little more
or show you stability in three bedrooms,
and looking back, you wouldn't see
smoke stacks or the front door.

## august rain

plucking courage
from somewhere
she's months into
this newest illness
still working still
somehow smiling,
everything passes
in grey sheets then
crumbles like yoyo
or a long landslide,
i'm awed, holding a
tub of vicks at the
bedside just giving
my brave face and
though it's wearing
out, there isn't any
thing else i have so
we make do with
that and settle into
sheets that smell so
much of eucalypt.

# beached

so I do miss the sea

it's taken nearly three years
to figure it out,
landlocked in a kind of dust
that pillows thirst

and thinking
often of seagulls doing
everything they can
to ruin a lunch
of salty chips and packet
sauce

I even think about
cuttlefish surfing
the afterlife and tiger
shells that always
seemed worth collecting
on school trips

or the tide
murmuring at night,
a parade of foam
warring with the shore.

## shell

I've turned my back on it and
turned up the music,
like in a quintessential
road movie.

as evening sun paints
the sky a pink
very close to tomorrow,
the letterbox
gives up our names.

the man who
came to raid the
lemon tree watches
as exhaust melts
the air.

our house is a shell again,
not precious
and beach-like, just
a knock for someone else to answer.

# **bianca**

on the bus
two girls talk baby names.

bianca
is popular

and I wonder if
they know it's italian for 'white'

and if they do
which 'white' do they have in mind?

is it the morphine
white of hospital walls
or the hard-working
plastic poly pipe
nestled beneath the sink?

could it be white like rabbits, robes
and weatherboard,

or milk and snow?
is it the white of a cloud
racing across sky

clever-marketing-ploy-white
of their iPods

or is it cherry blossoms nestled
against pink in spring?

## farm

dawn comes like someone embarrassed
to bring bad news, sunlight
very soft on weatherboard.

in the horse's mouth even straw sleeps
and the earth holds perfume,
memory of rain on pine needles.

hills are bone-grey and a cold hand
massages the empty river, no prayers
swim this belly of dust,
no whispers to quicken fruit.

night looks down in a shower of moth wings,
headlights turn powerlines into silver webs
and cheeks go unshaven.

## **woodsmoke**

afterwards I stand on the veranda
woodsmoke and rain
beading on the ferns
and nothing else

inside she's dressing for the trip,
hands smelling of milk and olive
and cheeks ready to fake a smile

it's possible to apologise
right up until we get into the car
but I don't because
somehow I'm convinced
that I'm defending myself

and it's the silence that pulls us down
fills my throat with fur
turns her skin soap-dry,
as rain beats a pattern on the roof
and nothing else.

## slow moon

out of the night
a slow moon
drips onto the driveway

his cloud-hat
lost back there somewhere
drifting
in the black-pupil sky,
his beams like
sagging tent ropes
while far below, patches of frost
sparkle on leaves

and he's too tired
to take them back.

## **mushrooms**

at the edge of the cemetery
where bolt cutters
opened a vein in the fence,
mushrooms
spread in obvious gestures
of bravery

and where else
would soil be so fertile, beneath
grass and tubes of bark
there lies an Iliad
of unfinished dreams

something of their
verve must seep into earth
must not go to waste, as countless
Achilles' could rise and stand;
now without pain, now
without heels.

## the pull of engines

1.
the road is burning copper,
lanes lost in rock-river, sun
feeding a steel empire
glass eyes roving
in moving cages,
hands glued to wheels.

2.
at the eighth floor desk
I'm writing;
turned my back on the window
on the airport, on
lights blinking
'sos' in multicolour
and engines egging each other on.

3.
just before the flight
hands twitch
on dry pages.

4.
only words can be revisited
with any clarity – certainly not
images
like car-chase butterflies.

5.
from the air the world is a red blanket
with charcoal dots
bunched up, like ants meeting
then scattered
when wind ruffles the sheet

when we dip low enough the roads
are military straight,
deep stencils
from a pen of fire.

## overlook

is it easier
for great poets
to romanticise their towns
when paris is rome is
new york is
london is berlin
is it easier
for them than my home

with street corners and marigolds
painted in vomit

industrial-strength
cigars, puffing second-hand
smoke into the sky

three inland surf shops
dozens of bars, six fast-food chains
and one theatre

is it easier?
maybe not, but I'd ask them
to find a moment
worthy of haiku,
where sewerage
and the paper mill meet.

## tar and white paint

   beside the road
   poppies in a red tangle
   and fish scales
   fluttering

   at my feet an old hook
   wedged between
   tar and white paint

   from the river
   the echo of our fishing trips
   and dark lines
   polishing the shore.

## harold

he once
raked autumn leaves
with tender hands

twilight
painted on white hair

and thick frames
desert farming,

from the green armchair
he watched me play soccer
with wooden men

cheekbones
and trousers creased

he stood
at the stove
and emptied his pipe.

## small town

has an old Esso sign on a tin shed
and someone who used to sell honey
painted yellow on the next one,

at the corner a pink golf ball
towers over the coastline, ridges
like the moon.

in spring flowers grow
round the blue tractor
and dirt collects in the seat

marks on the footpath
don't fade and the cemetery
never shrinks, only the town around it.

beyond the tennis courts
ghosts shed fingernails and
police sirens skip over fences;

no-one lives down there
where the surf plays dead
and moonlight walks on water.

## leaking

we're charcoal pressure
        along a white line - lights roll by -
  so happy so far
        the rags come too, we
  give the clock a head start this time
glove and gun, snap
   and snap, shop and stock

 it's only 9:30 but 6am is too close already
               and god i love her but
                   she hurts and i can't fix everything
       myself / what can i do for her face

                          when it falls
              to the floor
        sweep and cradle / milk in the
  morning and guilt with TV, chariots bursting
  into flames of red rose, the arms of athens
(crushing white)
  heave over the bowl
        in middle of the road, going for ok
        but not really there, slipping and calling
butterfly blinking
        watching me unpack with little twitches
of pollen, gold rainbows / in the mirrors
better teeth than i dealt myself

                [like a deck of 2s - the wine
       is sour in his hands where the cup sways

          where the garden opens - snepo - tuo]
& at once
  the pressure
comes again, a hand on the back of my neck
  cat's paw ripping up the walls / white rice
        going clear
and the deep blue of carpet
        sucking up all the smiles all the music
leaking
        leaving        leaking
                leaking        leaving

## late night

I know there's no way to stand out –

and it's very easy
to make someone's throat clench
with piano
and montage or a bit of slow
motion, soundtrack
really makes
up for substance

but what have I got – just lines
on white
envy
and really, why bother when
everything is so obviously impermanent

I guess the great lie of our time is capture –
it's comforting to believe
everything can be caught, recorded
and remembered,
so we don't have to appreciate
anything in the moment.

## sunrise today

it's a great way to get the conservative vote:
de-sexualise children
and crucify artists, have one right-wing
bigot applaud another
on a vile talk-show
that offers 'insights'
on hard hitting issues, that tells us
how to invest our 'spare' money
and tells how much chocolate is too much and
shows us how great consumerism can be,
by sending some cliché to paris
and having her shop
for slave-labour fabrics and a range of cosmetics
designed to deny change,
and show us please, yet another all-important
battle of the sexes
because if the world needs to know anything,
it's that gender is always about competition
and never about cooperation.

## it would be unfair to say

it would be unfair to say
wyeth had crippled christina

just as it would be unfair to say
that van gogh's clouds
are too milky

or saturn's appetite didn't
terrify even goya

it would be unfair to say
that monet's haystacks
must be softer
than any other

it would be unfair to say
waterhouse's lady of shallot
is simply too clean
for a woman roughing it
in a marsh

it would be unfair to say
the sailors
in hokusai's great wave
are not rowing
hard enough

and it would be unfair to say
klimt's judith is a flimsy
mask for a whore's
blush.

## how green wood burns

in the street someone
is burning green wood again
and around the corner
down by the highway,
that guy with a stall
beside the road
is selling confederate flags

another local gives me the eye
because he thinks that
he's a patriot
and again,
the woman in the library
grumbles when I ask
who is the best dry cleaner in town

it's almost a time warp
nestled just a few kilometres off the freeway,
like slipping back again
into a place based on
the history of segregation,
as found in movies or textbooks

but it's not colour or language
it's just that I'm new
again
and missus from the post office
doesn't know my father
and mister from the bank,
his son doesn't know me

something about this place
makes you want to lock
doors again, even
after the third check,
but not because you're worried about
dick and perry
but because you've bought into
the paranoia.

## on the road

when you're driving
you don't think about what they'd find,
what they'd call
'personal effects'
if they found your body.

in a pad full of notes
from other crash sites

you'd maybe be:

black-rimmed glasses
hair just-cut
wedding ring
and silver watch,
a few empty water bottles on the floor
pegs, a collection of john forbes' poetry
purple suit-jacket
last year's crumpled registration sticker
and a golf club in the back,
the one you found in the front garden
one morning

and all you are now
is a question (is this guy a donor?)
or a sheet to be filled out
at the morgue

you don't ask yourself, when driving
what kind of jokes they'd make about you,

it might be just like tv,
maybe they'd think you should have had
your prescription checked

and which one tells your wife,
how do they decide? will they draw straws
plucked from a roadside littered
with windshield glass?
or maybe rock paper scissors,
maybe it's just a job
to them, same way your job
is just a job sometimes.

when you're driving
you don't think about
how, on the way there, they might
get back to whatever it was they were
on about before the call,
could be Carlton getting a thrashing
last night
whether Australia should boycott
Beijing, or a girl
the driver's just met, he likes her legs
and she's into acting

you don't think about
yourself just behind the glass
in the supposed repose of the white sheet,
belongings in a plastic bag:
one that's somehow meant to sum you up
or give comfort to loved ones,
as if whatever happened to be in your car
the day you died,
would be everything
to the people who'd just lost you.

## october

when you sleep it isn't
hard to imagine you happy,
imagine that beneath hair
just washed
your jaw isn't clenched

and I do. I see a woman
who lifts my heart
with only her voice,
even diluted by miles
of telephone wire
and roads of black silk

even silent, against this doorframe
where the moment leans,
I see you waiting for spring
with a smile that I can't
possibly have imagined.

## **moonlight**

every now and then
if you listen close enough
particularly
pianissimo
you may hear the squeak
of a bench and know
that music is physical, even
in softest moments.

## little frontiers

gravel crunches in the lane
and plum trees
spread bloody-shadows
across lawns

streetlights interfere
with the moon
and bugs cross little frontiers

even this late
jasmine fills the air
and the echo of cicadas
brings afternoon to mind.

## alpine road

down from camp oven gap
bald hills of yellow grass
and ragged treetops
with bluesmoke buds

on the road a deer and her fawn,
bursting the wire fence,
gone in a scissor of legs

rocks sit in a muddy riverbed
round and smooth, like giant frogs,
their bellies bloated with death

and back on the mountain
mist no-one can catch.

## kakashi

that empty face,
hat curling in the breeze
and arms very broken

the coat is blood-blister
black and its ridges
are soft, as evening
draws shadow, and
round the crops

at absent feet,
brown leaves suffer
and buttons catch no light.

## take five

it's night and everything is sweating
me, the chair
the hand on the wall
keys
fingernails
headphone wire
supple black  V  round my neck
carpet sweats
and and and I'm bobbing my head
there's panic
underwater air so sloth
as I type
making up the world as I go
de-capitalising everything
keys jammed
beads ganging up on my back
and december rotting away outside,
I'm blood-tired/out-preening mirrors
stuck in the traffic
in my head in the vessels in the
skull in the temple empty
in the barely meadow
sunny blue flowers stunted sway
a collection
of soft stones
the snare, piano
chipping woodpecker hopping home
at lights out
alto drifts on wind
and sweats

(refrain)
now the fingers like potatoes
and knees
where they grow on the floor
rabbit
and make excuses,
now the glasses slip
oil slick
nose
and now the AM murmurs
adjusts, returns.

## fujin's bag

it's nearly 1am,
she's going to stir soon
and go for water
or the bathroom,
and outside the fern
will lean into frosted glass
and shake green fists
in a wind deep
enough to fill
fujin's bag
and I'm still moulded
to the desk, blinking
back sleep, convincing
myself, somehow
that all this
darkness is necessary.

## white butterfly

in the hallway
a white butterfly
swims through
forty-degree heat,
getting closer to the floor
with every desperate
pump,
and I cannot explain
sadness with words
alone.

## dive-bombing

inside you
there's something
that can go on
but only like a fluorescent light
flickers, and
remembers in jangles

and the more I try
to feed it with
words
in slow motion
dive-bombing
post-wedding confetti,
the darker it goes

and here I am with
fire-blanket hands,
wishing you could burn again,
but smothering the spark
with every
good intention.

## ashoka

whatever hands may wash
we will steal and muffle with boxes,
rachel's blue rose on the wall
armies
of cups, crippled toothpaste
and the
peter pan complex

only the body moves,
and thoughts stick
between
sills and taps that drip.

## orion's belt

as if god flicked a razor
against the window, last drops
from where he'd shaved white
from storm-clouds,
and left a lead bowl in place of sky,
a slight breeze
to carry scents from
stone picnics and exhaust fumes

for ants crossing the street
there was a red sea, traffic lights like alien
invasions and horns making thunder
in many colours
cars
rumbling
windows-down
men tapping
chili fingers on doors
blowing smoke
into air
beside the bakery
where brass savouries
mince about behind glass

the puddles gathered
like mirrors put up to something unpleasant
wavy, suffering blue, mixed with oil spots that
spread rainbow wings
and burst on the undersides of engines

so clever of the barber to think
of an umbrella
as he waits for the bus,
gutters crowding ankles
with the mob-rule of debris;
leaves, bottle caps
plastic wrappers and cigarette buts
rafting to the drain
and the sea-side
where swimmers
sunbathe

at night he'd look down at the hole
he made, one mighty fingernail
tearing the sheet and the saucepan
the only constant,
just six stars to cook dreams.

# echidna

it was sunday and god was resting
while somewhere back home, you wept
over the steel in your arm

I took a walk along the cliffs
and watched the sea tear itself
into a million black squids.

## black comedy

the trouble with harry
reminds me of matriciana now,
and when doing the dishes
in orange water
letting it grow
cold because I can't stop
thinking, about butterflies
and those short
months; don't the best of them
still have time to do whatever it is
insects do? the trouble with
dying is that it couldn't
ever be as funny as a black comedy

or will I, in fact, be able
to laugh at my body as it's lowered into a hole,
for some reason
in a suit in a box with
a pillow and my teeth probably
very clean and maybe
whitened too,
in case wherever I'm going
I'd need a great smile?

## bukowski and a wide range of landlords

some struggles are truly epic
like bukowski
and a wide range of landlords

or the hopeless
but well-meaning sign, painted
officious red

no alcohol in the CBD

and beneath it a smashed
VB bottle
coloured like a rotting
SA uniform

and my brother
snickering as we walk by

tastes like piss.

## eastern avenue

moon's hangover
hits the street in a splash of white,
outside the window
the transformer
is like a gargoyle, sitting
halfway up the electricity pole,
either too old
or too lazy to climb higher.

## bitches brew

words drove him through ash tray hills
rolling by half-lame spirits
robed in holy blue

he was worried, the liar, his
golden arms
unwrapping
leather straps round the mule

hands anchors
cities
blood-red in bottles
of midnight, sipping the smog
and ladies' perfume

skyline
a panther's arc.

sometimes, he went up, swirling with the wish-
wash of
hallucination; stars
cracking into each other like marbles
hurled by swollen knuckles

once, at the gate,
bragging about loneliness
he made a bow out of blue ribbon
and hung it above her headstone
murmuring to the wind.

## autumn-house

the slow decay of my neighbour's house
is something like going bald.
all night and all day the porch light is on
and while no-one can afford
to repair the window, paint the walls
or rescue the garden from the suburban
amazon it's become,
electricity seems to be free

but a semblance of life remains, the kids
still get to school (most days) and despite
operatic shouting matches to drown
out even the climax of nessun dorma, these
people and their autumn-house hold together

whether it's debt or love, it's
good to see him kiss her forehead,
leaving for work, thermos under one arm
and a smile not quite lost in stubble.

## botanic

1.
the park is full of photographers
and readers
ibis with black noses
and people who won't smile at me
and people who will

cicadas and crickets in hymn

a chinese couple
posing for wedding photos

by the river
and a fig tree that weeps
to the earth, medusa
in shackles of green.

2.
beyond the gardens
sirens tunnel through air

and streets hum with threats,
the casino is purple

and sandals
meet ash as leaves
tickle street signs

plum-soft
rain

and sunlight,
spread across buildings
dapple gentle
on brows
a monsoon of small change
trickling
in and out of vending machines
market stalls
and restaurants

while clear above them
construction
cranes make moves
while wind plays a mean
ballet with nests
while two 6s are stuck together
in a cafe
while deep in the river
lie bottles without caps
and bones of cod

then swiftly to shadows
in afternoon
where
bamboo stands together
full of gossip.

## royal on the park

at the hotel pool
reflections in chequered blue,
the fat boy circles
chairs
and at last disrobes,
each gesture a hip or an ankle

conscious of people in apartments
across the street
in a kind of rear window
montage:

a man opens a window
grunt riding
beads of sweat down his chin

a woman kicks thongs off
on the balcony her radio
stutters

a couple stare across the city,
letting go of whatever's
between them

and the boy
hovers in the deep end,
surrounded
by frangipanis.

## grass seeds

coming home
at night, stepping over
cherry blossoms
like scattered buttons, stepping over
seasons

there is no winter
in your house

everything has a kind
of dressing gown fuzz

where ugly thoughts can be
washed from hair
thick with
petrol fumes, or shaken out of
clothes like grass seeds.

## by the curve

a teacup sits on the sink
shoe-brown
inside, imagined marks
where you held it,
not by the handle
but by the curve, to fit a palm
aching from winter

and the rest of the kitchen
looks a little strained –
ant-killers nest against
the foggy window and
cutlery stands like a palisade

but somehow your teacup
shrugs off pain
with a sweeping shadow
cast low over the dish-rag,
to me it looks like you might
return at any minute.

## the jacket

on the chair
there's a filthy spring jacket
light enough
to catch every stray hair

a landscape
deep with ridges
from weeks spent crushed
into couch cushions, an ant might
spend a season in exile
dragging a single
crumb like penance

how important tomorrow
becomes, for the moses
of this desert is
your jacket, its pockets
full of stubs and receipts

I could map out
days and weeks, movies
you've seen, coffee
at hudson's and gelati
for summer

in the jacket
you linger in traces
and I rake them with my hands,
collect every scent.

# Author's Note

The following pages collect some of the pieces that were originally passed over when I compiled my first shortlist of around 100 poems, which I later narrowed down for what was first called *slow moon*.

By the time the collection became known as *Stepping over Seasons* I'd cut dozens and dozens for a second short list. There I continued to drop or replace older poems with newer ones until I came to a version of the collection fairly close to what was published in 2009.

Poems were left out for various reasons; often due to a similarity to other pieces which I felt, at the time, to be much stronger (*comes to rest, alice* for example.) Some works I removed because they didn't seem to fit the overall tone of the collection – such as 'cut-up' poem *little boy*. I seem to remember *scratching of birds* clinging to its spot in the running order until one of the final drafts of the MS.

Looking at the few I've chosen to replace now, I find there's some choices I still agree with but others not so much, which is part of the fun of looking back!

Hopefully they're just as fun to read and offer a slightly broader view of what else I was writing back then, along with a bit of insight into the selection process.

Ashley

## franchise

driving through a home town
has significance
until it becomes one of many

and now the state
seems crisscrossed with heart
strings that catch on the most
obvious things

street signs, greyed with mildew
rivers still polishing rocks,
creepers wrapping a water tower
and storefronts setting up smiles

all of it with a counterpart in another place
emotion under franchise,
about as special as hamburger meat
and looking like the copy of a copy.

## scratching of birds

why is it odd to see an old man
in Nike
on Anzac day

and why is toast so much better at night?

why do I miss the scratching of birds
on the roof
at 6am
now that they're gone

and what is it about the piano
about silence
that lets them meet
and wash every other sound
away, but gently?

## **nodes**

bamboo grew in our backyard
somehow
or I imagined it,
supple unforgiving
reliable, behind the shed
next to the pine
that towered over rusted
tools and number plates

maybe I remember bamboo or something like it
at school
could have been in a book at home,
one that I borrowed from school

somewhere I tried to break it
with a child's hands
with insane, destructive curiosity
I wondered
how pandas could eat bamboo

it was probably a movie
or a reed at the river, where we leapt
from stone towers like
infant gods
testing, stupid, happy
in summer, futureless
and unconcerned

the bamboo must have been
wicker curled into a washing basket
on mum's back step
or most likely something from
translation.

## little boy

territory denial and a man true to his mother

the shutter
is actually arranged to interrupt light
and the apple-worm is a pinkish-white finger

the poster may have said

until
a girl (and her doll) wearing pyjamas
was common to find in graves

Holst, Mars (06 August 1945 – present day)

crushing rail and pedestrian traffic
in a semi-autobiographical novel
by another confectioner's son

struck by a laundry truck
full of dirty atoms
an appetiser popularised in Manhattan
(does an oven mitt have a liver?)

whether you're looking for an inexpensive derby
or a legacy of bones

the only food colouring in the factory is pink.
Walter used it.

## cloudbank

in the movie
of their youth
he flashed
those piano teeth at her
and everyone thought
he'd come back

but now gulls plant
webbed feet by his hair

and the surf draws him
in, centimetre by
centimetre.

## signal

on the other end of the telephone wire
his punished face pleads
with words lifted from scriptwriters

peanut-birds watch, frozen
in the cheap pastel of evening
and streetlights sag like birth sacs, dragging his eyes
into puddles, hands waving
from cars, bikes and buses, all shuffling
down streets black with rain

he dials again, fingers shepherd numbers
out the window, into the city
and his body runs into the carpet,
soft as leaves settling.

## anything but cereal

part of me is waking up at ten to seven
and opening the gate
forcing myself to eat breakfast –
anything but cereal

and on the back step
where the laundry exhales
part of me plays a little guitar
till the fret wears down the 'e' string
and cuts my finger

part of me is throwing cds onto the backseat
and filling the car with petrol,
my atm card juvenile-blue,
wedding photo in wallet

and lunch something with cheese
as rain hits glass
with thousands of fingers,
very, very close to impolite

part of me is repeating these things
until I'm worn in
deep grooves
like a walking path over new grass,
until all that's left are flecks of
dreams like paint scraped
from walls.

## comes to rest

the dandelion clock
like a heart-beat fairy,
roams over
blackened trees
that reach from a seabed
of green,
frozen shipwrecks
spilling charcoal
from glorious wounds
and peppering
the sand,
each spore
thinner than mist,
comes to rest in
the smallest places.

# alice

a hammer took to the desert
and left everything in fragments,
but kept a place beneath a
winter sun, taking pains to be gentle

with scrub and ghost gums
exhaling, mud-coloured leaves
in the Todd, caught day-dreaming
a snake of yellow sherbet

gentle with ridges and rock faces
twisted, their noses broken and lips
swollen in frozen ochre,
raised like backs in a slow arc
to shave the sky
right down to spotless blue.

## Also by Ashley

*pollen and the storm*
*orion tips the suacepan*
*between giants/old stone*
*7 years*
*VI*

*nothing between
ghost-gums
but the wind*

www.ingramcontent.com/pod-product-compliance
Lightning Source LLC
Chambersburg PA
CBHW020703300426
44112CB00007B/490